Adult Coloring Stress Relief

with Calming Card Games

Clubs

Copyright © Leaves of Gold Press 2015

All rights reserved. No part of this book may be reproduced or transmitted by any person or entity (including Google, Amazon or similar organisations) in any form or by any means, electronic or mechanical, including photocopying, recording or by any information storage and retrieval system, without prior permission in writing from the publisher.

Creator: Leaves of Gold Press - author.

Title: Adult coloring stress relief with calming card games: clubs /
Leaves of Gold Press ;
Elizabeth Alger, illustrator.
Series: Adult coloring stress relief ; 5
ISBN: 9781925110890 (paperback)
Target Audience: Adult.

Image on reverse of cards: 'Pimpernel' by William Morris

BISAC categories:
Self-Help / Self-Management / Stress Management
Self-Help : Creativity
Body, Mind & Spirit / Mindfulness & Meditation

Scan the QR code to visit Leaves of Gold Press

ABN 67 099 575 078
PO Box 9113, Brighton, 3186, Victoria, Australia
www.leavesofgoldpress.com

CALMING CARD GAMES

Single-player games provide stress relief, mindful relaxation, fun and creativity.

This adult coloring book gives you beautiful, soothing designs on both sides of the cover and on the pages, to ease you into a state of relaxation. After you finish coloring, you can cut out the cards and use them to play simple, enjoyable card games for one player. These activities are designed to calm you down and help you recharge.

Each of the four books in the Calming Card Games series has enough space on the cover to create one suit of double-sided cards. Together they make a full deck of 52 (with a bonus 4 flamboyant jokers), hand-colored by you.

Card games require only a deck of cards and a flat surface, so they can easily be played almost anywhere.

Solitaire, also known as patience, is a group of card games that can be played by one person. Solitaire is absorbing and stress relieving. It also helps concentration and visual memory.

Why use real cards?

Playing games with real cards instead of on a screen makes a huge difference to your health. When you use virtual cards on a light-emitting screen your eyes may become strained. Even more seriously — especially in the evenings — the blue-wavelength light from screens interferes with your body's melatonin production, thus disrupting your natural sleep rhythms. Looking at a screen before bed not only makes it harder to fall asleep, but also affects how drowsy or alert you are the following day.[1] Digital solitaire can also be highly addictive, unlike real solitaire.

Play soothing games with real cards to relieve stress and get a better night's sleep.

Join the natural stress relief trends sweeping the globe!

---

1 *'Light-Emitting E-Readers Before Bedtime Can Adversely Impact Sleep.' Brigham and Women's Hospital. Proceedings of the National Academy of Sciences, December 22, 2014. Sleep deficiency has been linked to other health problems, including obesity, diabetes, and cardiovascular disease. Chronic melatonin suppression has also been associated with increased risk of certain cancers.*

THE SUIT OF CLUBS

The set of 52 French playing cards is the most popular European deck. This comprises thirteen numerals of each of the four French suits; clubs, diamonds, hearts and spades. Each suit includes three 'court' or 'face' cards; king, queen and jack.

The Suit of Clubs is derived from the Suit of Cudgels, or Batons. The French transformed them into *Trèfles* (clovers), sometimes called 'trefoils' in English.

In tarot, clubs corresponds to wands or sceptres. The element of wands is fire, and the Suit of Wands is associated with spirituality, inspiration, strength, intuition and creativity.

The Suit of Clubs represents the feudal class of farmers, laborers and peasants.

It also corresponds to the Swiss-German Suit of Acorns (*Eichel*).

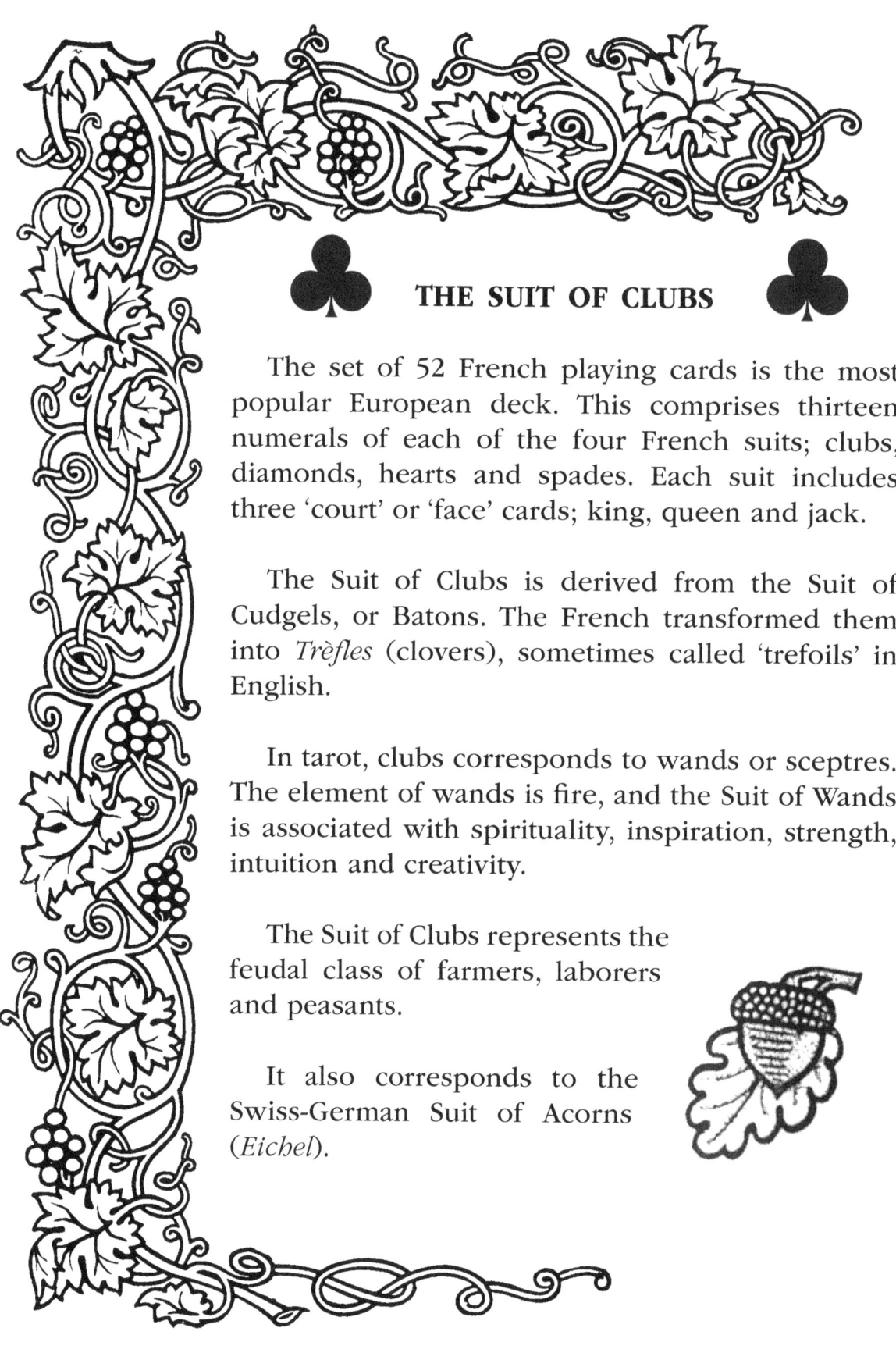

SOLITAIRE OR PATIENCE

Games of solitaire/patience generally involve re-arranging a layout of cards (called a 'tableau') with the aim of sorting them in some way.

There is a vast array of variations in one-player card games. The rules vary from simple to quite complex. Some use more than one deck of cards. This series of books, 'Adult Coloring Stress Relief with Calming Card Games' contains instructions for several of the most popular and relaxing games of solitaire, including:

- Klondike
- Accordion
- Flower Garden
- Spiderette
- Pyramid

Accordion Solitaire

If you play by the standard rules, it is not easy to win Accordion Solitaire. It can be a rewarding game, nonetheless, and helps hone your tactical skills. Because it can take a long time to play, Accordion is also known as Idle Year. Other names are Tower of Babel and Methuselah.

Instructions follow.

Suggested layout for Accordion Solitaire

ACCORDION SOLITAIRE

To play Accordion you only need one standard 52-card deck. The object of the game is to compress the entire deck into one pile, like an accordion.

Setup

A large table-top (or floor space) is required to play this game. First, shuffle the deck.

Next, spread out the whole deck of 52 cards face-up in a single row, making a tableau in which the cards overlap each other and every card's suit and rank is visible. Your row can be straight, circular or zig-zag. One suggested layout is shown opposite.

Gameplay

Aim to compress the tableau by matching cards according to suit or rank. You can place a card on top of the card immediately to its left, or on top of a card three positions to the left (meaning that there are two cards between the card you are moving and the card you are covering up), if the cards match in suit or rank.

When you move a card, along with it you must move any cards it was previously covering. Once you've covered a card, you're not allowed to uncover it.

Gaps left behind are filled by moving piles to the left.

Winning

The goal of Accordion Solitaire is to compress the entire deck into a single pile.

Helpful hint

Before you start playing, locate four cards with the same rank that are close together and near the end of the layout. Try to move the four cards to the end of the layout. Do not cover them with other cards (if possible) until the end of the game.

Variations of Accordion

- Some people like to lay out the cards face-up one at a time when they start the game, arranging them slowly. The benefit of this is that you can move a card straight away if you choose.

- Winning is almost impossible when you deal the cards one at a time and bring them into play as soon as you can. Since this is the case, Alfred Sheinwold in his book "101 Best Family Card Games" writes that if you use this variation you can be said to have won when there are five piles of cards or fewer left at the end of the game.

- To make the game easier to win, you can modify the rules to allow a card to be placed on top of cards in other positions. For example, you could allow a card to be placed on any of the three cards to its left.

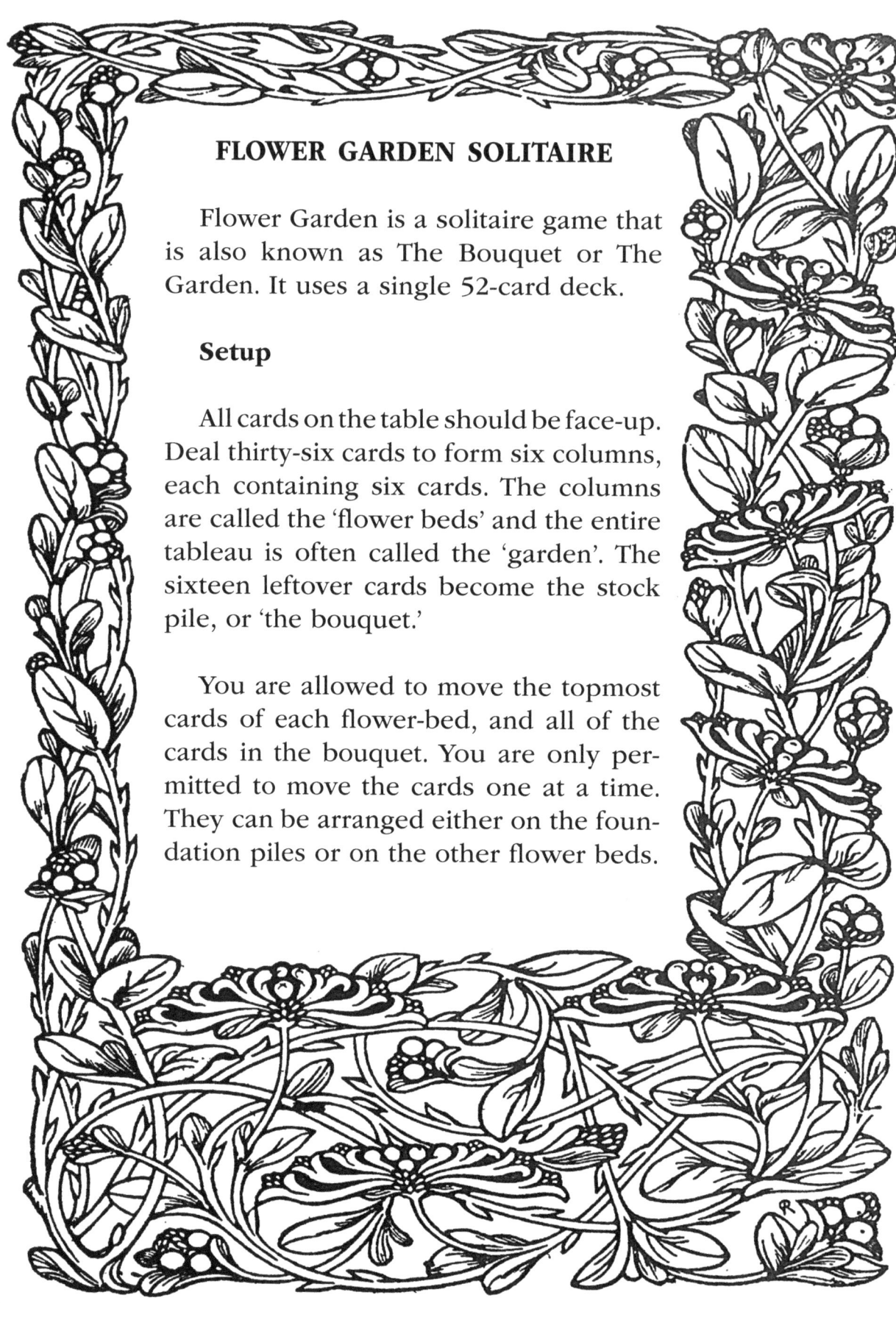

FLOWER GARDEN SOLITAIRE

Flower Garden is a solitaire game that is also known as The Bouquet or The Garden. It uses a single 52-card deck.

Setup

All cards on the table should be face-up. Deal thirty-six cards to form six columns, each containing six cards. The columns are called the 'flower beds' and the entire tableau is often called the 'garden'. The sixteen leftover cards become the stock pile, or 'the bouquet.'

You are allowed to move the topmost cards of each flower-bed, and all of the cards in the bouquet. You are only permitted to move the cards one at a time. They can be arranged either on the foundation piles or on the other flower beds.

Gameplay

Build up the foundation piles by suit, lowest to highest from ace to king. You should place the aces as the first cards on the bottom of the foundation piles.

The cards in the garden, by contrast, can be 'built down' (arranged in descending order) no matter what suit they are, and any empty flower bed can be filled with any card.

You can use the cards in the bouquet to help with building, to add to the foundations, or to fill an empty flower bed.

You win the game when you have placed all the cards in order on the foundation piles.

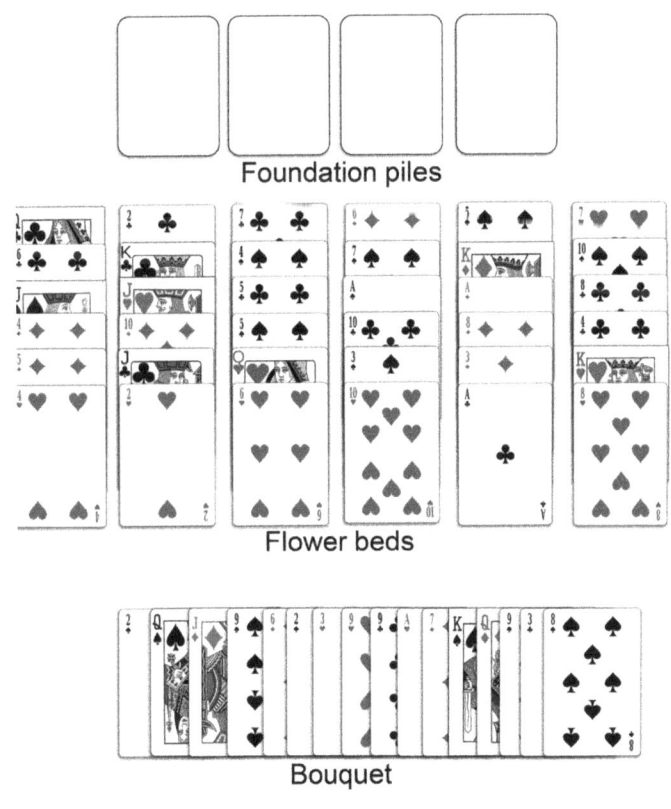

Layout for Flower Garden Solitaire

ADULT COLORING STRESS RELIEF: THE SERIES

Book 1: Adult Coloring Stress Relief with Calming Paper Crafts

Book 2: Adult Coloring Stress Relief with Calming Card Games: Spades

Book 3: Adult Coloring Stress Relief with Calming Card Games: Hearts

Book 4: Adult Coloring Stress Relief with Calming Card Games: Diamonds

Book 5: Adult Coloring Stress Relief with Calming Card Games: Clubs

IS FOOD MAKING YOU SICK?

People all over the world suffer from histamine intolerance without being aware of it.

We itch, sneeze, suffer from joint pain, inflammation, sleep disorders, irritability, anxiety, bowel disease, diarrhea, flatulence, stomach pain, heartburn and acid reflux, nausea, bloating and other digestive problems, eczema, psoriasis, tissue swelling, urticaria (hives), itching skin, itching scalp, sinusitis, runny nose, puffy eyes, hay fever, asthma, and breathing difficulties, or endure tension headaches, migraines, fuzzy thinking, dizziness, irregular heartbeat, painful periods (women), sudden drops in blood pressure, faintness or flushing.

Symptoms may endure throughout our entire lives if we continue to consume large amounts of histamine without knowing it. Histamine is colorless, odorless and tasteless — undetectable except by scientific analysis, and yet crucial to our well-being. Individual histamine tolerance thresholds vary greatly.

The good news is, if we can understand what is happening and why, we can treat or prevent this widely unrecognized condition. By far the best way to treat histamine intolerance (HIT) is with diet. All foods with the potential to raise histamine levels should be avoided until your health improves significantly.

This book discusses HIT in depth, including causes, symptoms and therapies, backed by scientific research. Along with a list of foods to help HIT sufferers, it includes a wide range of recipes for everything from entrées to desserts.

Find out more at www.low-histamine.com

THE SLEEP-INDUCING BEDTIME STORY

Children sometimes find it hard to get to sleep.

What if you could read them a bedtime story incorporating powerful psychological methods to help them fall asleep quickly, easily and without drugs?

Psychological sleep induction techniques include:
- putting aside your thoughts until the following day
- breathing deeply
- slowing down
- imagining a descent with the sensation of sinking
- progressive muscle relaxation
- using sleep-triggering words
- visualizing a safe and peaceful place
- employing the 'infectiousness' of yawning.

Such methods are well-known and can be found in libraries or by searching for 'psychological sleep techniques' on the Internet.

This book also uses the hypnotic power of rhyme and rhythm. Songs and lullabies have traditionally been used to lull children to sleep. 'Hypnotic' poetry works in much the same way.

The poems in this book are in the relaxing, calming rhythm called 3/4 time, better known as 'waltz time'. All parents know that gentle, rocking rhythms can soothe a child.

The rhyming is as important as the rhythm.

Children love poems that rhyme. For them, rhyming words make poetry fun and memorable. Just as children respond to Forssen Ehrlin's sleep-inducing story of Roger the Rabbit (the inspiration for this book), so they can fall asleep while listening to the tale of Misti the Kitty.

 # 1 New Release on Amazon in 'Sleep Disorders'.

www.ingramcontent.com/pod-product-compliance
Lightning Source LLC
LaVergne TN
LVHW070951070426
835507LV00030B/3490